IMAGES
of America

OGLEBAY PARK

BUILDING ON TRADITION. Local citizens have been returning to Oglebay Park for generations. They have created their own traditions here, which have helped to make Oglebay Park what it is today. Chase Herman (left) and his uncle Tim Parshall are fishing on Schenk Lake. Their family has been coming to Oglebay Park for five generations.

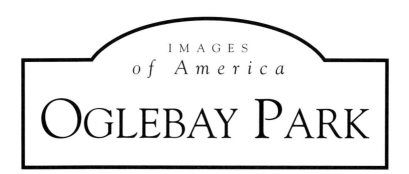

IMAGES

of America

OGLEBAY PARK

Brent Carney

Published by Arcadia Publishing
Charleston SC, Chicago IL, Portsmouth NH, San Francisco CA

Printed in Great Britain

Library of Congress Catalog Card Number: 2005920608

For all general information contact Arcadia Publishing at:
Telephone 843-853-2070
Fax 843-853-0044
E-mail sales@arcadiapublishing.com
For customer service and orders:
Toll-Free 1-888-313-2665

Visit us on the internet at http://www.arcadiapublishing.com

This book is dedicated to Philip Mayer Good, William Carney, and Sheila Carney.
All three loved Oglebay Park and made it a part of their lives and, in turn,
became a part of the park's rich legacy.

CONTENTS

ACKNOWLEDGMENTS

I am very grateful to Randolph Worls for his help with this project. Randy began working for Oglebay Park 50 years ago as a lifeguard and was superintendent/CEO of the Wheeling Park Commission for 28 years (1972–2000). He is now the president and chief executive officer of Oglebay Foundation. He is one of the many local people who have spent the better part of their lives insuring that Earl Oglebay's dream will continue.

I would also like to thank the following people and organizations in the production of this book: Doug Dalby; Mark Williams; Penny Miller; the Good family; Eric Mauck; Mary Lou Mauck; Ted Steckel; Ned Steckel; Barbara Palmer; Chris Schenkel; Holly McCluskey; Sue Weigand; Roxanne Wurtzbacher; Suzette Redford; Marc Harshman; Andy Barger; Jeanne Cobb; Eriks Janelsins; Connie Moore; Jeanette Gue; Frasier Smith; Ron LeMasters; Cathy Voellinger; Karen Waialae; Rod Haley; William Koegler; Jim Thornton; Nicholas Ghaphery Jr.; Dr. Alan Fawcett; Gary Zearott; Caren Knoyer; Ellen Dunable; Betty June Wymer; Robert Otten; Hydie Friend; Misty Ratcliff; Jennifer Shelburne; Rudy Agras; Ed Parshall; Joe Roxby; Anne Foreman; Gabriel Hays; Betsy Taggart; Robert Schramm; John Hargleroad; Steve Mitch; the Oglebay Foundation; Oglebay Institute; Wheeling Park Commission; *Wheeling News Register*; Wheeling National Heritage Area Corporation; Newbrough Photo; Our Lady of Lebanon Maronite Catholic Church; Hays Landscape Architecture Studio, Ltd.; and the T. W. Phillips Memorial Library.

Finally, I have to thank Travis Zeik, curator of the Museums of Oglebay Institute. Travis and I have collaborated on several projects in the past, and he has always been eager to share the Oglebay story with anyone who approached his office. He provided me with many hours of access to the Mansion Museum archives to find photographs and information for the captions. An overwhelming number of photographs used in this book were provided by the Museums of Oglebay Institute. Travis is truly an asset to Oglebay Park.

INTRODUCTION

Earl Williams Oglebay (1849–1926) became so successful in the iron-ore business that he was able to retire to his country estate, Waddington Farm, at the age of 51. Unlike some other Victorian titans of industry, Mr. Oglebay didn't just ensconce himself in his comfortable mansion. He built an avant-garde model farm that gathered world-renowned scientists to his estate. When he died in 1926, he willed his property to the City of Wheeling in the hopes that it would become a "people's park." Over the past 70 years, an army of volunteers, naturalists, artists, and generous local citizens have ensured that Mr. Oglebay's vision will continue. The Wheeling Park Commission (WPC), which owns and maintains all facilities and property in the park, has provided the leadership necessary to steer the park through the Great Depression, World War II, and several lean years. A separate, independent organization, Oglebay Institute, has provided cultural, educational, environmental, and recreational programming, which has helped to make Oglebay Park a special place. While researching this book, I was amazed at how many local citizens told me that their families had been coming to the park for three, four, and even five generations. All of these groups have helped Oglebay Park become the only self-sustaining municipal park in the United States and have brought Mr. Oglebay's dream to fruition.

One

Earl W. Oglebay

EARL W. OGLEBAY (1849–1926). In 1849, Earl Williams Oglebay was born in Bridgeport, Ohio, to Crispin Oglebay (1818–1871) and Caroline Rhodes (1819–1875). Earl's three brothers were Crispin (1859–1866), James (1846–1930), and Franklin (1852–1932). This bright young man grew to become more than just another multimillionaire. Colonel Oglebay is considered the father of Oglebay Park and was honored by West Virginia citizens as the "Most Useful Citizen of West Virginia" in 1915 as part of the Panama-Pacific Exposition. The region's citizens often tried to convince Earl Oglebay to run for public office, but he preferred to work his experimental farm.

BETHANY STUDENT. Earl Williams Oglebay was in the Neotrophian Literary Society while at Bethany College. Mr. Oglebay probably got the idea to purchase Waddington Farm when he passed it going to and from Bethany College along Route 88. Young Mr. Oglebay most likely learned many of his innovative farming practices while at Bethany College. Bethany founder, Alexander Campbell, was devoted to finding original solutions to agricultural problems facing Virginia's poor farmers. Oglebay was a popular student who never forgot his alma mater. His donations to Bethany College include the clock in the tower in 1904, the Oglebay Gates in 1910, and the Bethany College Farm in 1912.

OGLEBAY HALL OF AGRICULTURE, WEST VIRGINIA UNIVERSITY. Oglebay Hall was built in 1918 for the study of agriculture. It is listed on the National Register of Historic Buildings and houses several departments in the Eberly College of Arts and Sciences. The mast in front of the building was on the USS *West Virginia*, which served during World War II. There is also a bell from the armored cruiser USS *West Virginia*, which served in World War I. The bell is rung by the Alpha Phi Omega service fraternity during significant events.

OGLEBAY GATES. The gates were put into place in 1910; Earl Oglebay provided the funding, and the gates are named for him. One of Bethany College's most cherished rituals is when students pass through Oglebay Gates into the college during matriculation and once more during commencement. The act is connected to the college seal that was designed by Professor Richardson in 1843. The motto on the seal is "Pharetram veritas, sed arcum Scientia donat," which means, "Science furnishes the bow by which the arrows of truth are directed." The bows and arrows arm students with a quality liberal arts education; by passing through the gates at commencement, they demonstrate being so armed.

OGLEBAY HALL. The Oglebay Hall of Agriculture was added to the Bethany College campus from 1911 to 1912 to replace Society Hall, which burned down in 1879. Oglebay Hall was constructed in the Tudor Gothic style. Bethany College founder Alexander Campbell believed that Gothic architecture best expressed the style and spirit of the new nation. He said, "The Gothic has been adopted as the style most fitly expressive of the inspiring nature of the Christian's aims and hopes."

FLOURMILL. This flourmill was owned by Crispin Oglebay and Sons and was located in Bridgeport, Ohio.

OGLEBAY NORTON COMPANY. The *Crispin Oglebay* was one of several large ships owned by the Oglebay Norton Company. It was operated by the Columbia Steamship Company and was christened on June 17, 1948. To learn more about the Oglebay Norton Company, the author would recommend *Oglebay Norton: 100 Years on the Great Lakes* by Harrie S. Taylor.

BUSINESS PARTNERS. In 1884, Earl Oglebay (left) began working for the Tuttle, Master Company in Cleveland and soon became a full partner. John D. Rockefeller was a bookkeeper for the same company some years before. By 1890, the company was called Oglebay Norton Company. The company was named after Earl W. Oglebay and business partner David Z. Norton, who are pictured here at Waddington Farm. They became leaders in the iron-ore business and operated many mines, steamship companies, as well as other interests.

COAL SCRIP. This coal scrip is from one of the mines owned by the Oglebay Norton Company. Miners were given scrip in advance of their wages to buy essentials and also to pay rent on the company-owned houses. The Oglebay Norton Company operated several coal mines, including the Castile Mine, Montreal Mine, St. James Mine, Reserve Mine, Norton Mine, Saginaw Mine, Brule Mine, and the Pigmy Mine.

RICHWOOD SEWELL COAL COMPANY. According to the Oglebay Norton Website (*oglebaynorton. org*), "On August 22, 1944, the company becomes manager and sales agent for the Burton Mine of Richwood Sewell Coal Company in Nicholas County in West Virginia's Fauley Field with the ability to produce 1500 tons of Sewell Coal daily and a reserve of 40 years."

MILLIONAIRES ROW. Earl Oglebay owned two different houses on Euclid Avenue in Cleveland. This street was nicknamed "Millionaires Row" because many of the country's wealthiest men lived side by side on this prestigious stretch of land. Mr. Oglebay was equally at home among the titans of industry as well as among Appalachian farmers. The Mansion Museum has a personal Christmas card from Herbert Hoover to Mr. and Mrs. Earl Oglebay.

THE INDUSTRIALIST. Earl Oglebay made millions in the iron-ore industry, but this was not the extent of his interests. He became the youngest bank president in the United States when he was elected as president of National Bank of West Virginia in 1876. In 1912, his alma mater, Bethany, gave him an honorary doctorate. He was elected as an honorary member of Phi Beta Kappa at West Virginia University and later received an honorary degree. Earl was appointed by Pres. Woodrow Wilson to be the State Food Administrator for West Virginia during World War I. By the age of 51, he had become so successful that he sold most of his iron-ore mines and returned to Wheeling.

EARL AND SALLIE. Earl Oglebay married Sallie Paull Howell in 1881. Sallie was born on February 16, 1856, to one of Wheeling's most prominent families. Earl and Sallie lived in Cleveland, Ohio, and had one daughter, Sarita Howell Oglebay. Many of Sallie Howell Oglebay's possessions are on display at the Mansion Museum. Sallie was such a petite figure that she had to stand on a box for this photograph.

CRISPIN OGLEBAY (1876–1949). Crispin Oglebay was the trusted nephew of Earl Oglebay and executor of his will. He was instrumental in convincing the City of Wheeling to accept the gift of Waddington Farm. During 1929 and 1930, Crispin brought in nationally known naturalists, educators, and scientists to find a unique programming vision for Oglebay Park. He wanted the park to be more than just picnic benches. The result was that Crispin became the catalyst behind the creation of Oglebay Institute. He was chairman of the Oglebay Norton Company from 1929 until 1949 and remained a major benefactor to Oglebay Park and Oglebay Institute. Upon his death in 1949, Crispin Oglebay left approximately half of his estate to Oglebay Park.

YOUNG SARITA (1882–1930). Sarita is pictured here with her St. Bernard on the porch of their Eighteenth Street and Euclid Avenue residence. Sarita was married to Mr. Courtney Burton Sr. on January 31, 1912, in Cleveland, Ohio. They had one child, Courtney Burton Jr., on October 29, 1912. Sarita was 5 feet, 10 inches tall. When her father died, Sarita donated sizeable funds to the city of Wheeling to help them convert Waddington Farm into Oglebay Park.

SARITA'S WEDDING, 1922. This snapshot shows the guests at the wedding of Sarita Oglebay Burton and Albert W. Russel at Waddington Farm in 1922. Sarita married her father's longtime friend, Albert, four years after the death of her first husband. Albert stands to the right of Sarita in this photo. The proud father, Earl Oglebay, stands to her left and is wearing a straw hat. Courtney Burton Jr. stands in front of his grandfather. Albert and Sarita lived in Cleveland and Gates Mills. The book *An American Legacy: The Oglebay Story*, by Isaac M. Flores, is a great source for information on the Oglebay family. According to Mr. Flores, Sarita purchased a clapboard house within view of a polo field in order that her son could be close to the sport he so loved.

COURTNEY BURTON JR. (1912–1992). Courtney Burton Jr. was the grandson of Earl Oglebay. He spent his boyhood summers at his grandfather Earl's summer estate, Waddington Farm. He was a champion polo player who loved riding his favorite horses around Oglebay Park. Mr. Burton was involved in over 15 different projects at Oglebay Park and remained an influential benefactor his entire life. He is seen here riding in a parade during Oglebayfest. In 1978, the WPC dedicated the hilltop area as the Burton Center in honor of Marguerite R. and Courtney Burton.

Two

WADDINGTON FARM

WADDINGTON FARM. This etching comes from *History of the Panhandle of West Virginia*, published in 1879. It is probably the earliest image of the mansion. The mansion was constructed in 1846 by Hanson Chapline. It was originally an eight-room farmhouse. Earl Oglebay purchased the mansion and 25 adjoining acres in 1900 and used it as his summer estate. He was the ninth owner of the mansion, and he renovated his beloved home. He continually purchased adjacent farms until, at the time of his death in 1926, Waddington Farm had grown to 750 acres. One can see the small barn on the left, which later became the Clubhouse.

THE ROAD TO WADDINGTON. Earl Oglebay was the 14th person to own the lands of Oglebay Park. The first 13 were as follows: Silas Zane (1780–1785), Joel Zane (1785–1812), Noah Linsly (1812–1814), Lancasterian Academy (1814–1816), Samuel Sprigg (1816–1846), Hanson Chapline (1846–1856), George Smith (1856–1864), Alexander Mitchell Jacob (1864–1869), William W. Miller (1869–1872), James Paxton (1872–1878), Frances E. Phillips (1878–1884), John L. Stroehlein (1884–1888), and A. Allen Howell and heirs (1888–1900). The Ohio County Public Library contains a wonderful book, *Oglebay Park: Owners of Lands of Oglebay Park from: Silas Zane to Earl Oglebay, 1780–1900*, by Audra Rickey Wayne. They have VHS tape of local re-enactors portraying each of the owners of Oglebay Park.

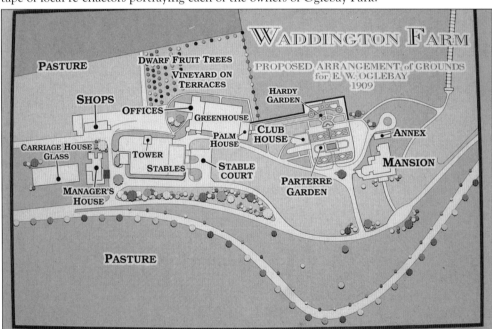

PLANS FOR WADDINGTON FARM. This drawing shows the early plans for the hilltop area at Waddington Farm. The world-renowned landscape architect Ossian Cole Simonds (1857–1931) designed the formal gardens. Mr. Simonds was one of the founding members of the American Society of Landscape Architects and wrote *Landscape Gardening* in 1930. He once stated that the landscape architect must be "a dreamer, a designer, an innovator, a creator—a dreamer more than most designers because it takes years for his designs to develop." Waddington Farm provided a perfect environment for such a visionary to experiment.

GATEHOUSE. Cottage No. 1, built in 1908, was one of at least three gatehouses around Waddington Farm. It had a large gate that was locked across Route 88 at night. This structure still stands and is inhabited by Chris Schenkel, director of horticulture.

"POLE-CAT RUN," 1906. This interesting photograph lists "Pole-Cat Run" as an entrance to Waddington Farm. It appears to be near the Falls Run Gatehouse. The English country-style gatehouse was built around 1902. The six-room structure once had a fireplace in every room. The Carriage House Glass assistant manager, Betsy Taggart, is the current occupant.

ROAD TO THE DAIRY FARM. The photographer is standing approximately where Schenk Lake sits today. Earl Oglebay's hope was to turn Waddington Farm into a model farm that would serve as a laboratory for new agricultural techniques that could be used to end the great starvation in the United States. He turned over parts of Waddington Farm to various researchers so that they could learn more about crop rotation, soil improvement, and cost-cutting methods.

FALLS RUN. This winding path was one of the ways to enter Waddington Farm at the beginning of the 20th century. The Falls Cottage Gatehouse sits out of view to the left of this picture. It was built around 1902.

VIEW OF GREENHOUSE COMPLEX. This view shows the north side of the greenhouse complex, c. 1910. Earl Oglebay's tree collection can be seen in the background. He brought over 150,000 trees to Waddington in order to create his arboretum. Sallie Oglebay was passionate about her greenhouse flowers and frequently had them shipped to her home in Cleveland.

GREENHOUSE, 1910. In the background one can see the wooden (steel reinforced) water tower. This tower used to have a bell, to signal the farmworkers, as well as sleeping quarters. Later, Mrs. D. A. Burt provided funds to purchase a carillon that was placed in the tower. Prof. Robert Schramm stated that when Edwin Steckel was executive director of Oglebay Institute, he would play the carillon sometimes during the day and on Sundays during vespers, which were held in the outdoor theater. Professor Schramm has a recording of the carillon, which he made on Christmas Day 1953.

ALFALFA FARMERS, 1915. Route 88 was built on a former cow path, which earned it the nickname "Cow Path to Culture." This alfalfa wagon is heading north on Route 88 and is preparing to turn into the gates of Waddington Farm. This photograph was taken at the top of Serpentine Drive, which no longer exists. Earl Oglebay introduced alfalfa to the northern panhandle of West Virginia and proved that alfalfa, in conjunction with lime, could reinvigorate depleted soil. The alfalfa fields covered what is now the Wilson Lodge area.

HAY FARMERS. Waddington Farm produced copious amounts of hay for the farm's horses. These rugged farmworkers are standing on a 30-foot mountain of hay. In 1961, Oglebay Park offered very popular hayrides that wound their way through the park. An Oglebay Park brochure stated, "Kerosene lanterns lend to the rustic atmosphere for organizations or Park guests who organize hayride parties." The ride cost 50¢ for kids under the age of 12.

FARM HAND. There were 15 different departments for farm operations at Waddington Farm. Each department was run by a separate manager. Earl Oglebay's plans for an innovative model farm required not only laborers, but also a host of progressive agriculturalists willing to put cutting-edge theories into practice. According to historian Anne Foreman, many of the farmers were initially skeptical of Oglebay's unconventional farming methods and considered him as a "man from the city trying outlandish things." Most were eventually won over by the results. More information on Oglebay's experimental farm can be found in *The Story of Oglebay Park* by Ralph Weir.

OGLEBAY WORKERS, 1915. These workers are posing at the farm manager's house. They are among the 75 men who worked at Waddington Farm. Earl Oglebay was distressed over the increasing infertility of the soil in West Virginia, so he hired a scientist and paid for him to travel to England in order to learn how the farmers there were able to continually improve each generation of crops. The scientist returned with theories about soil cultivation and crop rotation that served Waddington Farm well over the years.

SUMMER ON THE SOUTH LAWN, 1910. The photograph shows the Oglebays taking a summer stroll on the South Lawn. Mrs. Sallie Oglebay is carrying her parasol while Earl Oglebay is on the far right. Earl Oglebay's friend and business partner, David Z. Norton, is in the center with the mysterious black armband.

TEA ON THE PORCH. The Oglebays are taking an afternoon tea in the wicker furniture on the front porch. The front porch was added to the mansion in 1905. This was considered a living space, which was routinely used for tea parties. Earl Oglebay spent much of his time, and took many of his suppers, on the front porch.

WEDDING PARTY, 1922. The Oglebay family is seen here at the wedding of Sarita Howell Oglebay Burton and Albert Russel. Earl Oglebay can be seen in the center with a straw hat and dark jacket. He has his hand in his pocket. Sarita's son, Courtney Jr., is sitting in front of Earl Oglebay.

EGYPT ROOM, 1910. The Oglebays had this room in the clubhouse renovated in the Egyptian style following a trip to North Africa. The wicker furniture and gaudy furnishings were considered to be very sophisticated during the Victorian age. The clubhouse was designed in the Greek Revival style, and the Egyptian Revival interior was seen as a natural complement.

THE MANSION. This view of the mansion shows the beautiful porches (now removed) before the Burton wing was added. Notice the small sign to the left of the photograph.

THE PERGOLA. This 300-foot-long grape arbor stood on the ridge to the southwest of the mansion. It was built in 1905 and was removed in 1940.

PANORAMIC VIEW, c. 1915. This classic photograph shows some of the farm shops to the far left of the image. The greenhouse, water tower, and guesthouse are just behind the shops. The carriage barn and quadrangle, both destroyed by fire in 1965, are partially visible. The farm manager's house, vegetable gardens, and the boardinghouse are also seen. The Old Inn can be seen where Mr. and Mrs. Black lived. They fed the farm workers in alphabetical order.

HILLTOP AREA, c. 1910. This view shows the mansion, greenhouses, fruit trees, a rose garden, water tower, stables, and the carriage house. Today this area comprises part of the Brooks E. Wigginton Arboretum. The 90-acre Arboretum area includes a terraced garden, walking paths, and the watershed area around Schenk Lake.

THE FORMAL GARDEN. Shortly after Mr. Oglebay purchased the property, he began work on his spacious gardens. This formal English sunken garden contained a lily pond, a teahouse, and fine floral displays. Notice the boys with knickers and the large lily pads in the pond. Many of Wheeling's couples choose to get married on this beautiful spot.

THE DAIRY FARM, c. 1910. The dairy farm housed a prized herd of Guernsey cattle. It had a creamery and workers' housing. It was destroyed by fire, but its foundations were used to construct the children's center. Waddington Farm also had a poultry farm, a pig farm, and a sheep farm.

ARRIVING AT THE MANSION, 1915. Courtney Burton Sr. and Courtney Burton Jr. are seen here with their horse, Lady Grey. Horses must have been a constant sight at Waddington Farm. Mr. Oglebay used them not only as a means of transportation, but also for breeding and competition. His love of horses produced many champion horses and an equestrian tradition that is still alive today at Oglebay Park. Courtney Burton Sr. died from influenza in 1919.

CARRIAGE HOUSE. Pittsburgh brewer George W. Smith built this structure in 1856 as a carriage house. George W. Smith gave the name Waddington to the entire estate because his country home in England was called Waddington Heath. The park used it as a museum of travel until it was destroyed in a fire in 1965. The museum contained a Conestoga wagon, sleigh, carriages, and other antiques at the time of the fire.

BORDER RAIDER. In 1912, Earl Oglebay brought a famous Guernsey bull, Border Raider, from England. Over 8,000 people came to the Border Raider Guernsey Breeder's Association auction held at Waddington Farm to bid on Border Raider's Victory Maid. One can read more about Border Raider in Isaac M. Flores's book, *American Legacy: The Oglebay Story.* Border Raider was a famous figure in the world of animal husbandry. He and one of his "wives" were featured in the March 1926 issue of *Field Illustrated* magazine, in which they were described in flowery language.

BORDER'S BABES. This photograph shows the daughters of Oglebay's famous bull, Border Raider. Border Raider sired 30 daughters by the age of 11. According to historian Anne Foreman, 19 of Border Raider's daughters produced over 100,000 pounds of milk per year and were famous for their "well-shaped udders." Earl Oglebay chose his Guernsey bloodstock from the Isle of Guernsey. He spared no expense in bringing the finest cattle to Oglebay.

Three

PLACES IN THE PARK

HEADLINES. Upon Earl Oglebay's death in 1926, he willed his estate to the people of Wheeling as long as they "shall operate it for public recreation." It took almost two years for the City to finally decide to accept the estate in July 1928. The City had just opened Wheeling Park, and they were not sure that they could undertake the operation of a new park. Fortunately, H. G. Ogden, a local newspaper owner, and other citizens helped to convince the City of the park's worth. The Wheeling Park Commission and Crispin Oglebay also deserve much credit for helping to persuade the city elders that Oglebay Park would be a place of research, culture, and learning, as well as a place to picnic. The trustees of the Sarita Oglebay Russel Fund made the early years at Oglebay Park easier by providing three loans for construction projects in the park. The trustees provided a $51,000 loan for the swimming pool (1936), an additional $49,000 loan for the pool (1937), and a $15,000 loan for Camp Russel (1939). These loans collected a five percent interest. Today, Oglebay Park is the only self-sustaining municipal park in the United States.

TYPICAL CABIN, OGLEBAY PARK, WHEELING, W. VA.

TYPICAL CABIN. During the Great Depression, federal funds became available through the Works Progress Administration (WPA) to build several facilities at Oglebay Park. The Civilian Conservation Corps (CCC) created Camp Waddington (1936–1941) and aided skilled workers in the construction of the Crispin Center, cabins, a golf course, an outdoor theater, a swimming pool, trails, and roads in the park. The first cabins were constructed from discarded utility poles that were found by Mrs. Florence Fawcett. At one time there were 26 cabins in the park, and they were all named after trees with a different letter of the alphabet. Cabin X was so named because they couldn't find a tree beginning with the letter X.

HERB GARDEN. The Herb Garden behind the Palm Room is a cool spot to sit and relax. The Wheeling Garden Center was formed in 1938 to promote interest in horticulture and to serve as an information center for local gardeners. This is just one of the many clean, quiet places in the park. It could be one of the reasons that the *Charleston Daily Mail* said, "The first and last thing that strikes us is that it isn't just clean—it's immaculate."

FORMAL GARDEN. This religious ceremony at the formal gardens was not out of place in the early years at the park. The *Clevelander Magazine* noted, "Recreation, Culture, and Religion—All are had at Oglebay Park."

THE SILO. The children are studying in front of the silo, which was once a part of the dairy barn at Waddington Farm. The park was the site of the Waddington Peoples College from December 1, 1927, to March 1, 1928. This enterprise was sponsored by the Oglebay Estate and the West Virginia University Agricultural Extension Division. According to *How Waddington Farm Became Oglebay Park,* "The school was designed primarily for young people who had not had college experience but who wished to become acquainted in an informal way with literature, history, psychology, music, dramatics, handicraft, and various recreational activities."

NATURE MUSEUM. The first Nature Museum was in the "pink parlor" in the mansion. In 1930, it was moved into the Carriage Barn, as shown in this photo. Structures such as this needed much maintenance now that the farm had become Oglebay Park. The WPC was created earlier on January 26, 1925. This governing, umbrella organization develops, owns, and maintains all facilities within Oglebay Park. A WPC amendment declared that "any other parks hereafter acquired by the city of Wheeling, either by gift or purchase" would be controlled by the WPC. Many of Wheeling's most prominent citizens have served on the WPC in order to see that both Wheeling Park and Oglebay Park would be well funded and maintained. Former commissioner Sam L. Good retired from the WPC in 1973 after serving for 40 years, with 19 of them as chairman.

WILSON LODGE. Wilson Lodge is considered the centerpiece of Oglebay. The original rooms of Wilson Lodge were built in 1957 and the dining room was added a year later. It was named in honor of William P. Wilson, a friend of Earl Oglebay and a charter member of the WPC. It now has 212 rooms, and over 50 rooms are being added. It attracts over 200,000 visitors and serves over 400,000 meals per year.

SWIMMING POOL. This pool is part of the Crispin Center and is adjacent to the 18-hole Crispin Golf Course. The pool measures 75 by 65 feet, with an adjoining wading pool that opened in August 1937. Both Buster Crabbe and Johnny Weismuller swam in this pool during a visit. The center was constructed by skilled laborers with the help of the WPA and the CCC. Oglebay superintendent Homer Fish was in charge of the workers and was not above getting his own hands dirty. Dr. Alan Fawcett was one of the first lifeguards at the pool, and he stated, "Homer Fish would never ask you to do anything that he wouldn't do himself."

HORSE SHOW RIDING AREA. The show ring was added to the Oglebay Riding Academy in 1952. This postcard shows how popular the shows were among Wheeling's citizens. The ring has been the site of numerous competitions and has been home to several champion equestrians.

Riding Academy — Oglebay Park, Wheeling, W. Va.

RIDING STABLES. The Oglebay Saddle Club was started in 1929 and led to a more permanent Oglebay Riding Academy in 1931. This academy was first located in the Crispin Center area near where the tennis courts sit. Ground was broken for new stables in the autumn of 1946. The new academy was dedicated in 1948. These stables were made possible through a generous grant from the H. J. Heinz Corporate Foundation.

AERIAL VIEW OF CRISPIN CENTER. This 1941 aerial view of the Crispin Center shows the Brown Farm, which is above and to the right of the white house at the top of the photograph. The old Speidel Farm can be seen in the upper left-hand side of the photograph to the left of Route 88. The photograph also shows the site of the old riding stables near the site of the present tennis courts. The spherical parking lot is currently the site of an athletic field. This image comes from eight-time Emmy-winning producer, Ned Steckel, who stills lives in the white house seen in the photo. Notice the lack of houses and trees around Mr. Steckel's home.

AERIAL VIEW OF SKI SLOPE, JANUARY 1969. This view shows the ski slopes, the driving range, and a piece of the par-three golf course.

SCHENK LAKE. Oglebay's Schenk Lake is actually two man-made lakes. The largest was created in 1953 and was made possible by sizable donations from Albert Schenk III. It was named in honor of his parents, Albert F. and Frances Schenk. The Schenk Lake Boathouse was added in 1955. Only artificial lures are allowed on the upper lake, while bait can be used on the lower lake. A 26-inch trout was recently caught on the lower lake.

STOCKING SCHENK LAKE. This photograph was taken by a photographer from the *Wheeling News Register* on May 17, 1956. The lake is stocked with trout, catfish, bass, crappie, and bluegill. It is also home to many snapping turtles, ducks, swans, and geese.

40

Four

THE ARTS

OGLEBAY INSTITUTE ACTIVITIES COMMITTEE. Founded in 1930, Oglebay Institute provides cultural, educational, environmental, and recreational programming for personal and professional growth. The five areas that encompass Oglebay Institute are the Museums of Oglebay Institute, the Stifel Fine Arts Center, the School of Dance, Towngate Theatre & Cinema, and the Schrader Environmental Education Center.

FESTIVAL OF NATIONS, 1930. The back of this photograph reads, "Participants in the annual Festival of Nations on July 4, at Oglebay Park. Ten nationalities are represented in the group, which presented the folk songs and dances of its representative units. Exhibits of 'arts and crafts of the Homelands' in the Mansion Museum have become increasingly interesting and beautiful 'by-products' of Oglebay Institute's work with Americans of foreign descent."

REGIONAL MEN'S CHOIR, 1935. The back of this photograph reads, "Front Row Sitting, (L to R), Frank Sanders, Director; Clarence Stricklin, Gen'l Farmer; Leonard Rowley, Hazel-Atlas; J. E. Romine, Ohio Co. Agent. 2nd Row (L to R), Rev. Dykhuizen, Minister; John Hunter, Dairy Farmer; Donald Powell, Gen'l Farmer; L. E. Crow, Mgr. Whg. News; Fred Herman, Gen'l Farmer; Ralph Hunter, Dairy Farmer; Ralph Clovis, Carpenter; M. J. Orr, Dairy Farmer. Four men on Piano (L to R), Sam Reynolds, Bakery; Ralph Bergner, Warwick China; Frank Rowley, Hazel-Atlas; Harry Lydick, Rural Teacher. Back Row (L to R), J. A. McCutcheon, Poultryman; E. C. Atkinson, Dairy Farmer; Harold Bergner, Hazel-Atlas; George Flouer, Continental Can; Wm. Orr, Bookkeeper; Wm. Cox, Carpenter; C. W. Orr, Dairy Farmer; Robert J. White, Gen'l Farmer; Leo Tighe, Truck Driver; Thomas Orr, Landscape Gardener."

CREEK PAINTING. Oglebay Institute and the Nature Center often held painting classes out in natural settings.

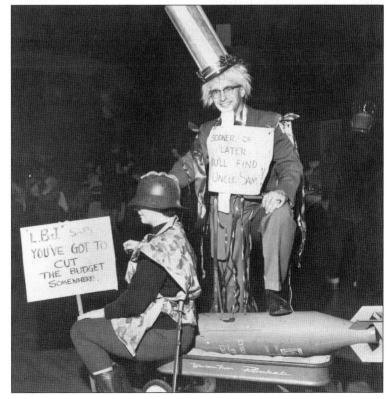

BEAUX ARTS BALL, 1964. This tongue-in-cheek production poked a little harmless fun at President Johnson.

"ROUND THE MAYPOLE," LATE 1930S. May Day was often celebrated by singing and dancing in circles around a maypole festooned with brightly colored ribbons. According to Emmy-winning producer Ned Steckel, many of the ideas used by Oglebay Institute came from studying the Chautauqua Festival of southwestern New York State. The group was formed in 1874 and held an annual nine-week Chautauqua Festival. This summer festival taught a diverse range of subjects including music, nature conservation, and crafts.

CHILDREN'S THEATRE, c. 1930S. This children's play is set on a stage in the Carriage Barn. The children are performing this skit as part of their Oglebay Day Camp activities.

CLOWNS. The children are performing a balancing act for a large audience.

"MUSICADE," 1945. Oglebay Institute brought in experts in different fields to teach specific classes. For example, Boris Goldovsky came to Oglebay each summer for a number of years to instruct locals in opera performance. This photograph was taken by Edward A. Martin.

PATRIOTIC DISPLAY, c. 1942. This photograph shows a civilian defense play at the amphitheater. The Oglebay Institute began as a collection of volunteer committees and produced a variety of different musical performances at Oglebay Park. According to historian Barbara Palmer in her book, *For Everyone Forever: The Story of Oglebay,* "The Wheeling Symphony Orchestra actually started as an outgrowth of the music committee, delighting the public with concerts at the park as early as 1929."

SHAKESPEARE IN THE PARK, JULY 4, 1929. This play was one of hundreds sponsored by Oglebay Institute over the years. The back of the photograph called the event "Theater in the Woods."

MIKADO GIRLS. These young ladies are participating in the Oglebay Youth Camp.

THE MIKADO, 1938. The Tri-State Musical Association Inc. and the Wheeling Symphony Orchestra performed Gilbert and Sullivan's *Mikado* at Oglebay's Amphitheatre on Tuesday, June 21 through Wednesday, June 22, 1938. The amphitheater was built in 1936 by skilled workers and with help from the CCC. Over the years, it has been the site of hundreds of plays and recitals. Thousands of Wheeling's citizens have been entertained here under the stars by performers such as Victor Borge, Steve Allen, Robert Merrill, Benny Goodman, Count Basie, and Louis Armstrong. The amphitheater was recently renamed for Anne Kuchinka, who donated funds for lighting and seating.

MUSEUMS
OF OGLEBAY INSTITUTE

Oglebay Institute
WHEELING, WV

Inspiring the Imagination

OGLEBAY INSTITUTE.
Oglebay Institute, the
largest private arts
organization in West
Virginia, annually offers
more than a dozen major
exhibitions, 75 music and
theater performances,
special events, camping
and nature programs, and
350 classes, workshops, and
seminars covering a broad
spectrum of the arts and
cultural and environmental
education topics. Theater
has been a part of Oglebay
Institute's programming
since its inception in
1930. What began as
"Theater in the Woods"
is now Towngate Theatre,
which was purchased by
the Institute in 1970. This
church-turned-theater,
located in Wheeling's
historic Centre Market
District, is home to a full
season of community
theater productions.

Five

NATURE

THOREAU TRAIL. The famed naturalist Alonzo Beecher Brooks led daily walks through the scenic trails of Oglebay Park. A. B., as he was known, established the Nature Leaders' Training School, which was the first of its kind in the country. Here he taught an entire generation of environmentalists his deeply religious and hands-on approach to nature. The Brooks Bird Club, named after him, has over 1,000 members in more than 10 countries. A. B. is a member of the Wheeling Hall of Fame and the West Virginia Agriculture and Forestry Hall of Fame.

At the beginning of the Thoreau Trail
A Sunday morning Hike

Sunday Bird Walk. A. B. Brooks's walks made him a local celebrity and well respected throughout the environmental community. In 1911, the book *Forestry and Wood Industries* stated, "A. B. Brooks was among the greatest of West Virginia's naturalists."

TRAILSIDE ZOO. The park's first zoo was behind the dairy silo, roughly where the miniature golf course is today. It contained some small farm animals and a few native species. This photograph is by Robert W. Schramm.

SNAKE STUDY. This Oglebay naturalist is looking at a snake skeleton inside the Brooks Nature Center. The center housed many skeletons and stuffed animals as well as live animals in small cages.

WINTER WALK, c. 1955. This is probably one of the winter bird counts held annually at Oglebay Park. This photograph shows how enthusiastic Wheeling's citizens were about participating in the nature programs at Oglebay Park. All of these people were willing to walk through the snow and cold just to learn about nature.

TRAIL CLASS. A. B. Brooks is seen here describing a pinnately compound leaf. He believed that the trails around Oglebay Park provided a natural classroom, and he took full advantage of them. Brooks's legacy has been the source of inspiration for three generations of naturalists. Prof. Jim Butler, Ph.D., of the University of Alberta, returned to the Shrader Center recently to discuss ornithology and the future of nature education. He stated that he considered Brooks to be "almost a deity" and that his career was simply an attempt to "walk in the footsteps of A. B. Brooks."

TELESCOPE TRUCK, c. 1947. The first telescope in Oglebay Park was located on Telescope Hill, where Wilson Lodge now sits. This Newtonian telescope had an eight-inch clock mirror drive and was cherished by the old Oglebay Astronomy Club. Much to their dismay, this telescope was ripped up and thrown into the trash dump. A second telescope, a Zeiss refractor telescope, was donated to Oglebay Institute by the Speidel family. This photograph shows the telescope being moved to its new location near the Nature Center.

SKY WATCHING, c. 1948. This photograph shows Fred Amos (far right) giving an astronomy lecture on Telescope Hill with an eight-inch telescope. Prof. Robert Schramm remembers that, between 1951 and 1955, the Astronomy Club would allow people to look through the telescope three times a week and that these sessions would regularly bring in over 200 people. The Benedum Planetarium will continue with the tradition of sky watching at Oglebay by holding Astronomy Day on April 16, 2005. David Holden will hold a telescope workshop, while others will conduct a workshop on making sundials.

SNAKE PIT, c. 1950s. The snake pit was an exciting place behind the old dairy silo where children could conquer their fear of reptiles under the guidance of park experts. Local non-venomous snakes were on view and could be handled once the children learned a few basic lessons from the herpetologist. These students are sitting along the rail and waiting impatiently for their turn to see a snake close-up.

TREE TUNNEL, MAY 15, 1932. These 4-H members are seen here distributing young trees to 5,000 children at the 1st Annual Arbor Day Celebration. More than 7,500 people attended this event. The Wheeling Civic Garden Center continues the tradition of tree planting by funding projects such as the introduction of crab apple trees above Schenk Lake in 1968.

ARBOR DAY, 1932. This is a photograph of a tree-planting ceremony at the Girl Scout Camp. The tradition of tree planting at the park so impressed the writer John W. Handlan that he wrote the following in an article for the August 1938 issue of *American Forest Magazine*: "A three-year old spruce tree is not an especially impressive object to the layman. It gains little in interest, in his eyes, when it is carefully removed from its nursery row and has its roots and slim, lower base neatly wrapped in moist, brown paper. But when it is assembled with 5,000 of its prototypes and made the center of a spectacular ceremony that same little tree acquires heroic dimensions."

NIGHT WALK, AUGUST 1927. A. B. Brooks is seen here conducting a night walk with some of his students. The young girl in front of A. B. with the dark jacket and white pants appears to be eating something. It could very well be some edible plant that A. B. pointed out along the trail. A. B. Brooks's distinct approach to nature compelled many to write nature poetry. Acclaimed writer Marc Harshman recently told the author that he continues to be inspired to compose poetry by the Brooks Nature Trails.

POWWOW, 1952. The back of this photograph reads, "Five Circle." These young boys were given a better appreciation of Native American food, medicine, and methods of hunting by participating in day camp.

IROQUOIS BURIAL MOUND. These young boys may be at the Oglebay Day Camp or members of the YMCA Indian Guide program. The author (Rising Sun), his father (Half Moon), and his brother (Shooting Star) all took American Indian names when they joined this organization in the early 1970s. They hiked through Oglebay, shot arrows, and learned a lot about nature and Native American culture.

TREE PLANTERS, 1933. The two children are participating in an Oglebay Arbor Day celebration. Enormous crowds would gather at Oglebay Park during these events. The entire hillside was covered with masses of local people.

A WELL-EARNED MEAL, 1927. Dorothy Parshall was one of the local citizens who relished A. B. Brooks's morning bird walks. She told me that there would usually be a home-cooked meal of bacon, eggs, and coffee waiting for the walkers at the trail's end. She recalled that the smell of the food was so vexing on the latter half of the walk that they would start to walk faster. A. B. would gently tease them that if they didn't pay attention to his lecture, he would slow the pace even further. Brooks's holistic approach to education encompassed your eyes, ears, nose, and mouth. Notice the knickers, boating hats, and pug-ugly hats.

MOZART SCHOOL WALKERS, C. 1930. Oglebay Institute has always been devoted to providing Wheeling's children with unique opportunities to learn about themselves through the study of nature. The Residential Environmental Education Program (R.E.E.P.) was established in the 1970s. This program brought local sixth graders to Camp Russel for one week, where they lived in dormitories. This photograph was taken by A. B. Brooks.

BILL BEATTY. The renowned nature photographer is seen here petting a stuffed great horned owl. Bill is a nationally recognized photographer who can frequently be seen hiking along the A. B. Brooks Discovery Trail System, focusing his lens on some small bird or shrub. In a recent interview, Bill stated, "A. B. Brooks is one of those rare figures whose influence and legacy actually changed the direction of people's lives." Bill's photographs have been featured in numerous magazines including *Audubon*, *Discover*, *Backpacker*, *National Geographic World*, *Natural History*, *Scientific*, *Nickelodeon*, and *Wonderful West Virginia*. Bill's website is http://users.1st.net/net/wild/gallery.html.

NATURE'S CHAPEL, 1928. A. B. Brooks points toward the sky during this outdoor lecture. He is probably pointing to a bird in the tree, but it's equally plausible that he was pointing toward heaven. A. B. Brooks was a deeply religious man who saw nature as proof of God's abundant goodness. The noted ornithologist Dr. Jim Butler told the author during an interview, "The birds were A. B. Brooks's choir."

WHEELING'S BUSINESS WOMEN, AUGUST 1927. The back of this photograph reads, "Wheeling's business and professional women having breakfast out-of-doors." A. B. Brooks took this photograph and was probably leading them on one of his nature walks. Mr. Brooks was an excellent photographer, and his camera is on display at the Schrader Center. Note the woman on the right who is chomping down on a piece of watermelon.

Announcing ~

The road to outdoor adventure. Students of the 1934 School prepare to explore Spruce-Pine Hollow in the Eastern, W. Va. Panhandle.

The Eighth Annual

NATURE TRAINING SCHOOL

at

Oglebay Park, Wheeling, West Va.

and

Randolph County, West Virginia

June 10 - July 2, 1935

A. B. BROOKS, Director

The Eighth Annual Nature Training School is sponsored by The West Virginia Nature Association, Inc. in cooperation with Oglebay Institute, The Agricultural Extension Division of West Virginia University, The Wheeling Park Commission.

NATURE TRAINING SCHOOL, 1935. This pamphlet for the Nature Training School shows that even back in 1935, Oglebay Institute was very disciplined about getting the message out to local citizens about the nature programs available at the park. The Nature Training School was started in 1927 and was directed by A. B. Brooks.

JUNIOR NATURE CAMP. The Junior Nature Camp was an extremely popular learning experience where children learned about nature through direct study. The column on the left-hand side of the brochure shows how every minute of every day was utilized in order to make the lessons of the camp last. The nature classes were often conducted by nationally known experts in their field, such as Dorothy Treat from the National Audubon Society.

Oglebay Institute
Junior Nature Camp News

CAMP RUSSEL, OGLEBAY PARK   WHEELING, W. VA.   JUNE 9 TO 15, 1963

JUNIOR NATURE CAMP SCHEDULED JUNE 9-15

"Jam-Packed" Daily Schedule Set at Camp

You probably want to know what goes on each day. The activities are varied and are a little different each day for the individual camper.

The sample schedule below will give you some idea of the daily pattern, but even that is broken with a mid-week special activities day. Something is planned for every minute, and there are always surprise guests and visitors.

Here's what your day will be like at Junior Nature Camp:

6:30 Rising Bell
7:00 Bird Walk
8:25 Flag Raising
8:30 Breakfast
9:30 Cabin and Area Clean-up
10:15 Swimming & Other activities
12:30 Let's Eat
1:30 Canteen open
2:00 F.O.B.(Flat on Back)
2:30 Outdoor activities
4:45 Recreation and free time
6:00 Wow! Time to EAT
7:45 Vespers
8:00 Campfire and Fun
9:30 Snack
9:45 P. J. Time
10:15 Lights Out

MAIL CALL, CANTEEN, BANK, LIBRARY HERE

CAMP CANTEEN. Open every day for a short period after lunch. Cards, stamps, books, candy, etc., will be for sale.

MAIL. Will be distributed every day in dining hall.

CAMP BANK. For your convenience and protection of valuables. LIBRARY. Books from the Koehnline Memorial Library will be available.

EVENING ACTIVITIES. Vespers, campfires, stunts, special programs, snacks.

CLOSE TO NATURE

DESPITE RISING COSTS JUNIOR NATURE CAMP TOTAL FEES REMAIN SAME

Despite rising costs, you will be glad to know that Junior Nature Camp fee remains the same as the past several years. Your total cost of $30.00 for the whole week even includes health and accident insurance. When you send your application that is printed on Page 2 you include with it a deposit of $5.00. The balance of your fee is due upon your arrival for official registration at camp.

Be sure your application blank and $5.00 are sent in by May 15. Deposit fees are not refundable after May 31.

If you care to you can pay the full amount with application, or some campers find it convenient to forward half the fee and pay the balance at camp.

SCHOLARSHIPS AVAILABLE

Two nature camp scholarship funds under trusteeship of Oglebay Institute have been set up to help deserving boys and girls and young adults. In the past, each year, several campers attending Junior Nature Camp at Oglebay Park and the Nature Leaders Training session at the Mountain Camp, Terra Alta, have received assistance.

More recently, the Joseph H. Bruning Memorial Fund was created from contributions made by friends of the late Mr. Bruning. The amount of the scholarship varies each year with the number of applicants. Partial scholar-

ships from 1/3 to 1/2 the camp fee are available.

The main requirement in being considered a candidate is a genuine interest in nature study. If you are in Scouting (Boy or Girl), 4-H or other groups that have conservation and nature programs and projects, it will be counted in your favor.

If you are interested — become a candidate. You have nothing to lose, everything to gain — write for information and application blank for camp scholarship to: Nature Education Department, Oglebay Institute, Wheeling, West Virginia.

Camp Russel Site of 1963 Encampment

Oglebay Institute's Junior Nature Camp will be in session from Sunday, June 9 to Saturday, June 15 at Oglebay Park's Camp Russel, Wheeling, West Virginia. Camp will open officially with registration at 3:00 p.m. (DST) June 9 and continue through Saturday, 10:30 a.m. Final date for enrollment is May 15.

Junior Nature Camp is open to boys and girls from 6th to 11th grade level. The Camp schedule and activities are geared for youngsters 11 to 15 years of age.

Planned especially for those who enjoy nature and life in the outdoors, this week-long camp is fun-packed with many particular activities, field trips and hikes, crafts and recreation. Beautiful Oglebay Park provides ideal surroundings and a memorable vacation.

Leaders who know the outdoors will guide exploring parties and other sessions. In addition, nature campers will enjoy popular games, swimming, campfires and special activities.

From early morn 'til lights out Junior Nature Camp will be filled with fun and action. Plan now to start your summer vacation at the Junior Nature Camp.

USE RUSTIC CABINS

Campers will be housed in rustic shelter-type cabins surrounded by a touch of wilderness. Central bath houses are nearby. A large log building overlooking a spacious playing field and rolling hills serves as dining room and assembly hall.

A counselor will supervise each group of eight campers.

HANDS-ON LEARNING, c. 1954. The Oglebay Nature leader is holding an American alligator, while the young girls are handling two non-venomous black rat snakes. They are in the Oglebay snake pit.

BEE KEEPER, JUNE 11, 1981. Oglebay Park once had its own beekeeper, Steve Paesani, who instructed students on how to safely make organic honey. Mr. Paesani worked in the midst of 10,000 bees.

TERRA ALTA. The Terra Alta Mountain Camp was founded in 1929 by A. B. Brooks to serve as a training ground for naturalists. The camp includes 18 acres of habitat for rare orchids, ferns, flowering spurge, warblers, thrushes, kinglets, and vireos. The camp provides classes for the novice as well as the professional naturalist. The daily schedule might include morning bird walks, canoeing, fishing, and classes in botany, herpetology, ornithology, geology, mammalogy, and macro-invertebrates. Terra Alta is located in eastern West Virginia, just southeast of Morgantown. A new Koehnline Lodge has replaced the original structures.

HOW TO KNOW THE PLANTS. These are two of the dozens of nature brochures that can be found at the archives at the Mansion Museum. They demonstrate how the Nature Education Department got the word out to local citizens about their many programs.

BUTTERFLY CLUB. These boys are probably local Boy Scouts trying to earn a merit badge. The Boy Scouts of America have made good use of Oglebay Park over the years.

PLANTING CEREMONY. The back of this photograph reads, "The official planters formally dedicate Ohio Valley tree plantings of 1932 to the memory of George Washington. The ceremony occurred during the first annual Ohio Valley Arbor Day celebration at Oglebay Park on May 15, 1932. Chairman Lee Spillers, of the Wheeling Committee on the Washington Bicentennial, takes his turn at planting while Chairman Otto Schenk of the Wheeling Park Commission (left) and Mayor-Manager Thomas Beckett, of Wheeling, look on."

BROOKS E. WIGGINTON, F.A.S.L.A. (1912–1995). Brooks E. Wigginton was the beloved, longtime landscape architect at Oglebay Park. Among his many design accomplishments are the garden center, par-three golf area, and the Good Children's Zoo. He also designed the walking trails, terraced gardens, and area around Schenk Lake. The current WPC director of planning, Andy Barger, stated that Mr. Wigginton had "a very good eye for seeing how structures could be placed in the landscape to take advantage of the vista or keep them hidden from view by trees. He always tried to maintain a lot of green space." In 1950, Mr. Wigginton was named to the Fellow American Academy in Rome and the Fellow American Society of Landscape Architects (F.A.S.L.A.) in 1958. He wrote many publications and penned a popular series of Victory Garden articles for the *Wheeling News Register* during World War II. In 1981, the 90-acre arboretum at Oglebay was named for Brooks E. Wigginton. Andy Barger remembers Mr. Wigginton as "a patient, thoughtful mentor."

Six

FAMILY FUN

CASCADING WATERS. This floating fountain sprays water to a height of 150 feet. This popular display attracts large crowds for nightly shows during the summer. The fountain has two 75-horsepower pumps that circulate 3,500 gallons of water per minute. It uses 84 1,000-watt quartz lights of different colors. An 80,000-watt sound system adds to this powerful show. Oglebay Park bought the fountain from Hydro Dynamics in St. Louis.

WATERFALL FUN. These children are probably there for one of the nature day camps. The Schrader Center still conducts nature day camps. This year's camp includes programs with interesting titles such as Water Wonders, Home Sweet Home Planet, Righteous Reptiles and Awesome Amphibians, The Fantastic Fun of Forests and Flowers, Unearthing Our Heritage, Become a Biologist, Encounter Insects, Nature Olympics, Explore Aquatic Ecology, and Survey Birds and the Sky.

ROASTING MARSHMALLOWS. Notice how many marshmallows are being roasted over such a tiny campfire.

DAY CAMP, 1930. Today there are approximately 40 numbered picnic sites in Oglebay Park that can be reserved. The park rangers collect $5 for each site. The non-numbered sites are free and are on a first-come, first-serve basis. Note the advertisement on the box, which appears to read, "Angier's Emulsion with Hypophosphites Practically Tasteless."

PERIOD DRESSING, SUNDAY, JANUARY 1960. Mary Lou Cupp had a summer job inventorying the collections at the Mansion Museum and found this hand-embroidered silk dress. In April 2005, the author interviewed Mary Lou Mauck and found that, as a child, her family brought her to Oglebay Park every Sunday between Memorial Day and Labor Day. In turn, she and her husband, Ron Mauck, vacationed at the park every year in the summer. She remembers putting her kids in her backpack and walking the trails at Oglebay Park. Her tradition at Oglebay Park is continued by her son, Eric, who is now vice president of operations at Oglebay Park. Eric brings his two boys, Michael and Nathan, to the park regularly.

COURTNEY BURTON JR. A young Courtney Burton Jr. shows his patriotism during World War I in the backyard of his family home in Cleveland. Later, Courtney had some bad timing as he was on a dove-shooting expedition in Cuba at the same time that Fidel Castro was starting his revolution to oust the dictator Fulgencio Batista. Courtney and his friends were relaxing aboard the yacht *Nacoya* when they were boarded by Batista's grenade-carrying soldiers. The soldiers feared that the rich *yanquis* might be running guns for Castro. After finding no weapons, the soldiers were invited to have a few drinks, and they soon staggered home. Courtney left Cuba with no injuries other than a severe case of poison ivy.

THE LONG BOARD   H. BARNES

THE LONG BOARD. Earl Oglebay hoped to build a model farm that would be turned into a model park upon his death. The *New York Times* published an article on April 21, 1963, that showed a photograph of Oglebay Park with a headline reading, "Oglebay Park has been called the nation's model municipal park by park authorities throughout the nation." The writer from the *New York Times* seemed to feel that he had accomplished his task.

"AQUAGANZA," AUGUST 5–6, 1941. The Junior League Inc. sponsored this musical/aquatic extravaganza. It included synchronized swimmers (shown here), acrobatic divers, musical numbers, and comedy skits. The Musical Steelmakers also performed. A 100-foot stage and elaborate settings were created, and professional lighting was added for the evening productions. During one of the rehearsals, someone dropped an electric cable into the water, which gave the synchronized swimmers quite a jolt. Over 2,500 people attended the first night of the "Aquaganza."

JUNGLE GYM. These children are enjoying a Sunday afternoon frolicking at the Oglebay playground, which is behind the Hess Children's Shelter. Even a humble jungle-gym play set needs funds to ensure its upkeep. The Oglebay Foundation was chartered on January 23, 1996, as a nonprofit corporation devoted to the welfare and future development of Oglebay Park, Wheeling Park, and their affiliated organizations. The renovation of the Palmer Signature Golf Course, the ski area and reestablishment of skiing at Oglebay Park, and the opening of the Diana T. Ihlenfeld Technology and Communications Center at Wilson Lodge are just a few of the many projects that the Oglebay Foundation has undertaken.

STUDY GROUP, AUGUST 1931. The back of this photograph reads, "Family Camp Study Group." The early years were very busy at Oglebay Park. Just a partial list of groups that met at Oglebay Park between May 1927 and November 1933 includes the National Meeting of the American Country Life Association, Regional Boy Scout Executives Conference, Regional Recreation Directors Conference, State Meeting Presbyterian Synod and Synodical, Regional Park Conference, West Virginia Editors' State Conference, State Quota Club Convention, West Virginia Farm Bureau Insurance Agents, Regional Girl Scout Executives Conference, National Social Recreation Institute, State Meeting International Federation of Catholic Women's Alumnae, Ohio County Teachers' Institute, and the National Conference Extension Rural Sociologists. The book *How Waddington Farm Became Oglebay Park* lists 53 other groups that met during this time (not including the many groups that used the park for dinner meetings and one-day conferences).

HULA. These young hula performers seem to be enjoying the attention. The myriad of different events held at Oglebay Park make it almost impossible to tell why the girls in this unmarked photograph were visiting the park. Among the hundreds of events held at the park were an Easter Sunrise Service, the Tri-State Kennel Association Dog Show, annual turkey shoots, antiques shows, reunions, and chamber music concerts. The *Christian Science Monitor* once called Oglebay Park "a national prototype of regional resources for human renewal through recreation."

RING AROUND THE ROSIE. These day camp kids were being led by counselors Sally Friedrichs and Mary Ann Hess.

SACK RACE. Oglebay Park has been used for over seven decades as a safe place to hold picnics and outings. Since its inception in 1996, the Oglebay Foundation has been providing funds so that all children could come to the park, regardless of their economic situation. The "Access to the Parks" program funds over 2,000 children from Ohio County who normally could not afford it to use the park facilities for free.

EASTER EGG HUNT. Oglebay Park hosted annual Easter egg hunts through the 1930s. Note the girl's "flapper" hat and the boy's knickers.

RIDING THE RANGE. The *West Virginia Blue Book* called Oglebay Park "truly a people's park from its inception."

Sunday with the CCC. A worker from the CCC is helping a young girl plant a tree in Oglebay Park. In 1934, the Oglebay Arbor Day program used the Farm Women's Club, 4-H Clubs, and local social organizations to create a "tree minded" community.

CAMPFIRE SINGING, 1932. A. B. Brooks took this photograph of Campfire Girls singing and dancing around an unlit fire.

LUMBERJACKS. This lumberjack competition may have been a part of the Oglebayfest. This event was first held in 1978 to commemorate the park's 50th anniversary. This festival includes a country fair, a parade, fireworks, musical performances, and a plethora of crafters showing their wares and demonstrating their techniques.

TACKLE FOOTBALL. This football game is behind Camp Russel, which was named for Sarita Oglebay Burton Russel. It was constructed with help from the CCC and accommodates up to 258 people. A poultry farm was located on the land that became Camp Russel.

MAHRAJAN, 1953. This cultural festival was first held at Site 1 in Oglebay Park on May 20, 1933. The Mahrajan (which is a Lebanese word meaning festival) usually attracts over 3,000 people. The festival is sponsored by Our Lady of Lebanon Maronite Catholic Church. The present pastor is the Reverend Bakhos Chidiac. This year's festival will be held on August 14, 2005, again at Site 1.

HALLER SHELTER. Haller Shelter was built in 1937 and named for Louis F. Haller, a charter member of the Wheeling Park Commission. According to *How Waddington Farm Became Oglebay Park*, "For three seasons in 1928–1930 mammoth community picnics, sponsored by the Community Improvement Associations, were held on Memorial Day." Oglebay Park now hosts over 125,000 picnickers each year.

CAMP RUSSEL. Camp Russel was constructed in 1939 and served several generations as a youth camp. In 1963, Sen. Robert C. Byrd convinced the White House to approve a federal grant of $137,460 to make needed improvements at Camp Russel. Senator Byrd proclaimed, "I am most happy to have been a part of this activity which will do much for Oglebay in continuing it as the most outstanding park facility of its kind in the nation."

INDEPENDENCE DAY, 1932. The Playground Day Camp was designed to enable kids from "congested, polluted cities" to come and study outdoors at Oglebay Park. More than 1,500 children attended the Playground Camp in 1932. The fresh air and open fields were seen as a healthy break from the smoggy environment of West Virginia's coal and steel plants.

Seven

THE GOOD ZOO

PHILIP GOOD. The concept for the Good Zoo was conceived in 1971 by Laurance and Barbara Good as a memorial to their seven-year-old son, Philip Mayer Good. Philip was a joyous boy who loved visiting Oglebay Park and whose zest for life was contagious. When Philip died of a brain tumor at the age of seven, his grieving parents wanted to find a way to honor such a brave and spirited young boy. In 1972, generous monies from the Goods, the Wheeling Parks System Trust Fund, the Federal Appalachian Regional Planning Commission, and the Bureau of Outdoor Recreation established funds for the zoo. The local community became enamored with the Goods' idea and pledged generous funds. The Good Zoo was dedicated in 1976 and opened in May 1977.

GOOD ZOO CONSTRUCTION. The Goods expressed their hope for the zoo when they stated, "A little boy lived and a little boy died, and he was so loving and so loved. So too, then with thousands of other children. These especially unique relationships within families—between a child and his or her mother, father, sister and brother—make the world go around, spark our lives with meaning and affection." In 1995, the Good Zoo was named in author Allen Nyhuis's *Zoo Book: A Guide to America's Best*, as one of the top-10 children's zoos in the United States. It appears that the Goods' goal has been accomplished.

ACCREDITATION, MARCH 1986. The people in the photograph are, from left to right, Penny Miller, Ron Hobbs, John Hargleroad III, Robert Wagner, and Randy Worls. Robert Wagner was the executive director of the American Zoo and Aquarium Association, and he is presenting the Good Zoo with its accreditation. Penny Miller is currently director of the Good Zoo. Ron Hobbs is a Wheeling Park Commission board member. John Hargleroad III is the director of operations for Oglebay Park. Randy Worls is the president and CEO of the Oglebay Foundation. The 30-acre Good Zoo is West Virginia's only accredited zoo.

BEARS. The two bears at the Good Zoo are among the most popular animals with the children. However, even the bears can't compare to Pajama the llama for pure star power. In 1984, the zoo handlers believed that Pajama was lonely, so they started the "Llovely Llady Llama Fund" in order to raise funds to buy Pajama a mate. On July 20, 1984, Jim Carney, vice president of Elby's Restaurant, agreed to donate $1,000 to purchase "Monica" the female llama. The story was covered by USA Today on May 3, 1984.

FIVE GENERATIONS, JULY 2003. Chase Herman, age four, is the fifth generation of his family to enjoy Oglebay Park. His great-great-grandmother, Bertha Conner Imhoff, attended many functions at the nascent Oglebay Park. His great-grandmother, Dorothy Parshall, went on Sunday morning bird walks with A. B. Brooks. His grandmother, Thyra Parshall, met his grandfather, Edward Parshall, when the two of them worked at Wilson Lodge. His mother, Kim Herman, worked at Wilson Lodge, sang with the Young Patriots at the Anne Kuchinka Amphitheatre, and presented Courtney Burton Jr. with his birthday cake.

TRAIN DISPLAY. The O Gauge Lionel Train exhibit opened in 1981 and was conceived by Donald Busey, Steve Mitch, and Douglas Dalby. This train display cost $15,500 to build and took a total of 600 hours to complete. The set contains over 8,500 planted trees, 1.5 miles of wire, 700 feet of track, 106 gallons of water, and 2 tons of cement. The trains run 12 hours a day, nonstop.

BISON. The Good Zoo has been a home to hundreds of different species of animals, including a Komodo dragon, giraffes, red wolves, meerkats, tree shrews, cotton-top tamarins, sloths, giant fruit bats, chinchilla, albino alligators, white tigers, black bears, bison, river otters, and rattlesnakes. It began as a place for only North American species but now includes endangered species from around the world. The Good Zoo also holds zoo camps for children aged 4 to 16.

MASCOT. The Good Zoo features over 80 different species on 30 acres of land. The author remembers working as a docent at Oglebay Park in the late 1970s and learning to conquer his fear of snakes. This unique program trained young volunteers to work at the petting zoo and at other areas in the zoo. The docents had to be at least 12 years old and had to be recommended by their science teacher and then pass both a written test and an interview.

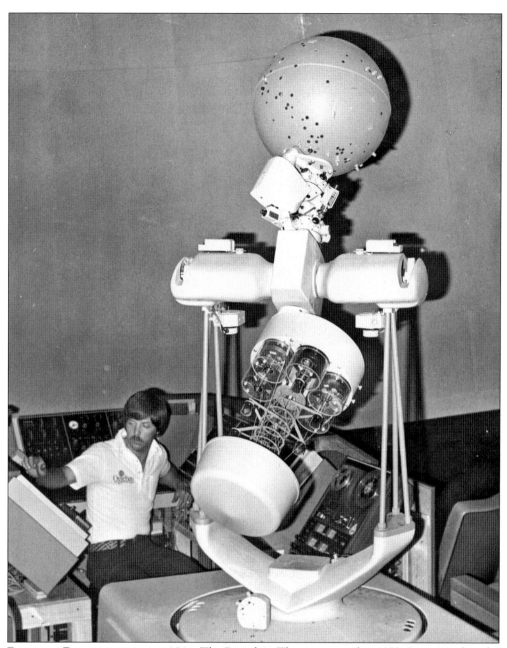

BENEDUM PLANETARIUM, c. 1970s. The Benedum Theatre opened in 1978. Steve Mitch is the man operating the Starfield Projector. He began working at Oglebay Park in 1966 and is now the director of the Benedum Planetarium and Natural Science Theater. The planetarium hosted the Pink Floyd Light Show in 1982 and also runs 35-millimeter versions of IMAX prints. *Ring World* is currently showing. The Benedum Planetarium is named after Claude Worthington Benedum in recognition of the generous support from the Claude Worthington Benedum Foundation.

RED BARN. The red barn has been at the Good Zoo since its opening. It is home to donkeys, a barn owl, and a pig. The Good Zoo has always tried to provide a safe and enjoyable place for children to encounter animals. Just outside this photograph to the left sits the goat-petting stables. Special events at the zoo include the Good Egg Treasure Hunt, Boo-at-the-Zoo, Farm Days, and Member Days.

ENGINEER ROCKEFELLER, MAY 28, 1977. Then governor John D. Rockefeller IV is driving the Good Zoo C. P. Huntington train through its one-and-a-half-mile course. Senator Rockefeller has remained a big supporter of Oglebay Park. He once stated, "Oglebay is becoming even more well-known, not only in West Virginia but outside the state, as a desirable year-round resort and recreational center. This has increased employment at Oglebay while pumping new dollars into the Wheeling economy."

Eight

SPORTS

FRONT NINE AT CRISPIN GOLF COURSE, c. 1935. The area around the Crispin Center was once used by grazing sheep. This front nine of the course was dedicated on July 4, 1930. Bob Biery laid out the plans for the Crispin Golf Course. Mr. Biery was inducted into the Wheeling Hall of Fame in 1984. This photograph was taken before the back nine was opened in 1938. For more than 50 years, the Bernhardts Amateur Classic was staged at Crispin. It is rumored that Border Raider is buried on the lower rough of the number-four hole at Crispin Golf Course.

CADDY CAMP, JULY 1931. This photograph shows a young caddy from the Oglebay Caddy Camp assisting three golfers. The Oglebay Caddy Camp began around 1931 under the direction of Bob Biery. The young boys involved in the program spent their summers living in bunkhouses where the CCC Camp Waddington once stood. The boys, ages 12 to 16, worked six days a week, and their earnings were kept in a bank account with $13 subtracted per week for room and board. Former general manager Randy Worls noted the benefits of the program saying, "There are few programs left where adolescents can be part of such an exemplary experience, where they can develop leadership skills and a good work ethic." *Junior Golf Magazine* once noted, "Two of the most noteworthy caddie development programs in the country are located in Wheeling, West Virginia and Cleveland, Ohio."

LPGA. The Robert Trent Jones Sr. course at the Speidel Golf Club was home to the West Virginia Ladies Professional Golf Association (LPGA) Classic from 1974 through 1984. The course struck fear into the hearts of many pros because of the hilly terrain and because the LPGA Classic was usually played in the stifling heat of mid-summer. Although its popularity remained constant, the prize money required by the LPGA grew beyond the means of the local community. This photograph shows Nancy Bunton chipping her way out of a sand trap during the 1980 LPGA Classic. One person was hit by lightning while standing near the old temporary clubhouse. He was given CPR by an Oglebay staff member and recovered from his injuries.

TOP OF THE SLOPES. The golfers on the green at the par-three golf course don't seem to notice that they are yards away from a young skier. This 18-hole course opened in 1962 and is a favorite with young locals learning the sport and with veterans just out for some fun. The longest hole is the par-three number 15 at 126 yards. The area around the par-three course was once a pig farm.

ARNOLD PALMER. Arnold Palmer visited his course to the delight of many of his fans. The par-71 Arnold Palmer Signature Golf Course ranges in distance between 6,800 yards from the championship tees to 4,200 yards from the forward tees. This challenging course opened in 2000. The 36 holes of golf at Oglebay Park may be one reason that the *Pittsburgh Post Gazette* said, "Oglebay may well be the ultimate park."

DRIVING RANGE, JULY 12, 1959. The Oglebay Driving Range opened in 1953 and has always been a favorite with golfers because it is sloped at a steep angle, which gives the ball a longer hang time. The driving range has 30 tees.

BURNING DOWN THE HOUSE, OCTOBER 27, 1997. This house and a barn were destroyed in order to build the Arnold Palmer Signature Golf Course. This course received four and a half stars from *Golf Digest Magazine*. According to historian Barbara Palmer, an official of the Palmer Design Company stated, "Because of the unique topography, it's one of the most interesting golf courses we've ever designed."

PUTT-PUTT. The miniature golf course opened in 1979 on roughly the same site as the Trailside Zoo.

CANOEING, 1987. These two intrepid explorers may not have journeyed as far as Lewis and Clark, but they appear to be having a great time on Schenk Lake. Oglebay Institute naturalist Greg Park will lead a canoeing expedition into the Canadian wilderness from August 7 to August 14, 2005.

SLALOM SKIING. This slalom course was behind the Crispin Center and appears to end dangerously close to the tree line. During the 1960s, Oglebay Park offered sleigh rides throughout the park. The sleigh was pulled by two horses and sat 12 people. The ride cost $1 per person. Frasier Smith took this photograph.

SKI JUMPING. This young man is on the ski slopes that cover the driving range during the winter months. Snowmaking equipment and a ski lift were introduced at the park in 1963 but were taken out of service *c.* 1994. A new ski lift and snowmaking equipment were reintroduced on December 18, 2004.

TUBING, JANUARY 2, 1981. The author can remember taking an inner tube from his father's garage and flying down the hillsides at Oglebay Park. Hundreds of others have the same idea every year.

VOLLEYBALL. This group was the senior girls' division of the Oglebay Institute's Day Camp. Miss Joanna Rogers was their counselor.

ISLAND JUMPING. These swimmers were enrolled in the Oglebay Day Camp. The back of this photograph lists the senior boys' leader as Bob Orlafske and the swimming counselor in the water as Mrs. Henrietta Scharf.

LIFEGUARDS, AUGUST 1941. Alan Fawcett (front) and Sam Bernard were among the first lifeguards at Oglebay Pool. Many of the boys were students in medical school who returned home each summer to make some money. In a recent interview, Dr. Fawcett told me that they made very little money but had a lot of fun. The record for a single day's attendance was over 3,600 people one summer day in 1940.

TARGET PRACTICE. These young men were learning how to safely use firearms at the shooting range in Oglebay Park. They were members of the Boy Scouts.

FORE! These two sportsmen are "playing" behind the Pine Room on October 24, 1960. I have no idea what caused these two men to be in the same photograph. It reminds me of the Monty Python Skit—"And now for something completely different!"

ARCHERY RANGE. These young men were probably participants in the Oglebay Day Camp.

TENNIS. The Jones Tennis Shelter was dedicated in 1953. It was named in honor of J. Sumner Jones, who was a charter park commissioner. It contains 11 Har-Tru tennis courts. The shelter includes the Dot Boll Memorial Lounge. Dorothy Boll was a popular local tennis player who won five West Virginia State Closed Women's titles. The shelter plays host to the Senior Tennis Tournament, Junior Tennis Tournament, and the West Virginia Open Tennis Tournament. Tennis great Arthur Ashe once played in a tournament at Oglebay early in his career. In 2001, the U.S. Tennis Association awarded the Wheeling-Oglebay Tennis Club as the Organization of the Year. John Chatlak, director of tennis, is giving lessons for tiny tots as well as advanced match play in the summer of 2005.

BASEBALL. This game took place at Camp Russel near the site of the chicken coops and poultry area.

HORSE JUMPING, AUGUST 1978. This photograph shows riders Randy Mullins and Melinda Kane practicing their jumps. Randy Mullins was the manager of the riding stables at the time this photo was taken. The photograph was taken by Frasier Smith.

THE HORSE SHOW. These elegant riders are entertaining the crowd from atop their champion thoroughbreds. This photograph was taken by Frasier Smith.

A DAY WITH THE HORSES. This photograph shows an equestrian event during the late 1930s.

Nine

THEN AND NOW

FISHING, THEN. This photograph shows George Breiding (far right) showing a young woman how to properly cast. Mr. Breiding was the director of the Brooks Nature Center from 1951 to 1963.

NATURE CENTER, THEN. The Brooks Nature Center was built in 1954 with funds provided by Courtney Burton Jr. and honors A. B. Brooks. Although the facility is no longer there, the ideals and spirit of A. B. Brooks are still very evident. A mission statement in the new center shows how little has really changed: "Our mission is to focus upon environmental awareness, appreciation, knowledge and action, while serving the advancement of environmental education to people of all ages on a local, regional, national and international scale. We hope through our efforts to develop informed and responsible Stewards of the Earth."

NATURE CENTER, NOW. Built in 2000, The Henry Stifel Schrader Environmental Education Center is considered one of the region's best examples of "green architecture." The building was made from 97 percent recycled materials and eco-building processes. The walls are made from 52 tons of the *Wheeling News Register*, and the flooring in the restrooms comes from bus and tractor tires. The ceiling tiles are made from volcanic ash, and the decking is made from recycled milk jugs and sawdust. Behind the Schrader Center are the A. B. Brooks Discovery Trail System, the Woodlawn Walkway, and the Joan Corson Butterfly Garden. Inside the center are the EarthTrek Exhibit Hall and the Children's Awareness Center.

GATEHOUSE, THEN. This English-style gatehouse was built *c.* 1906 and guarded the entrance to Serpentine Drive. This road was created for Mrs. Oglebay, as she did not enjoy riding along the steep and bumpy Route 88. The drive is no longer in use except by avid trekkers who enjoy the scenery.

GATEHOUSE, NOW. The gatehouse now sits along GC&P Road and is in need of repair. Many local historians are hoping that funds will be found to repair this historic structure. All three remaining gatehouses are worthy of attention and restoration. Most travelers along GC&P Road have no idea that the unique little structure even exists. Former Wilson Lodge chef Richard Reynolds and his wife, Sharon, live in the gatehouse. Richard has worked for the park for 35 years, and Sharon has been a groundskeeper for over 22 years.

PLAYING INDIANS, THEN. These young boys are attending the Oglebay Day Camp. The abundance of learning opportunities at Oglebay Park is just one reason that the park is the envy of much larger metropolitan areas. *The Pittsburgh Press* once asked, "Why can't we have an Oglebay."

PLAYING INDIANS, NOW. These men are reenacting a scene from the last battle of Fort Henry, Wheeling, in 1782. They are members of the 2002 Fort Henry Days Project, whose goal is "attempting to educate and enlighten the public as to the life and times of those who lived on the early frontier." The group uses approximately 300 volunteers and attracts over 2,000 spectators per day.

NATURE TRAIL, THEN. A. B. Brooks was the Oglebay naturalist from 1927 to 1942. The original Brooks Memorial Trail was dedicated on August 27, 1944. Brooks Hall at West Virginia University is named "in honor of the Brooks family of Upshur County whose sons have contributed extensively to West Virginia's biological research and to the state's biological literature." The brothers include Alonzo Beecher Brooks, Fred Ernest Brooks, Chandler Linn Brooks, and Earl Amos Brooks.

NATURE TRAIL, NOW. The A. B. Brooks Discovery Trail System includes three trails. The Falls Vista Trail is one mile long and takes one hour to complete. The Habitat Discovery Loop covers three-fifths of a mile and takes approximately 30 minutes to walk. The Hardwood Ridge Trail is two miles long and requires one and a half hours to hike.

SCHENK LAKE, THEN, MID-1950S. Notice the ice skaters on Schenk Lake. The original boathouse was much smaller than the one to come later. Also take notice of all the houses that are visible through the trees. They are no longer there. The warehouse on the left of the photograph was used to store equipment. Frasier Smith took this photograph.

SCHENK LAKE, NOW. This photograph was taken on April 5, 2005. The boathouse is much larger, and the platform for the Cascading Waters can be seen in the middle of the lake. Also notice the tunnel connecting Schenk Lake with the playground.

FARM MANAGER'S HOUSE, THEN. This structure was built in 1856. The porches and shed have been removed, and a road now crosses what was the front yard. Mr. Oglebay remodeled the residence with large porches (now removed). A recent addition to the back of the building was designed to conform to the style of the original structure.

FARM MANAGER'S HOUSE, NOW. This photograph shows Oglebay Park's Visitors' and Information Center and Wheeling Park Commission administrative offices. This building also contains the Christmas in the Gardens gift shop. Adjacent to this building is the Bissonnette Gardens. The gardens were named for Joseph F. Bissonnette, retired director of development for the WPC and former executive director of the Pittsburgh (Pennsylvania) Zoological Society. This 16-acre garden is a re-creation of gardens that existed in the early 1900s. It contains thousands of mums, tulips, daffodils, and hyacinths.

CLUBHOUSE, THEN. In the mid-1800s, a barn was raised on this spot. This barn can be seen in a few early images of the hilltop area. Earl Oglebay remodeled the barn into a clubhouse and guesthouse. This photograph shows the clubhouse after the second story was added. This clubhouse was a popular site, with recreation and game rooms on the first floor. The second floor had five guest rooms, a dinette, and a kitchenette.

CLUBHOUSE, NOW. The clubhouse is now called the Oglebay Institute Cultural Center. Dr. Perry Gresham, president-emeritus of Bethany College noted, "I have lived through the striking development of Oglebay. The acres are carefully planted and manicured; the buildings, which date back to the last century, have been assiduously maintained; the new buildings are of such excellent quality that Oglebay is now superior to most public parks in America."

MANSION, THEN. This photograph shows the mansion as it looked between 1884 and 1888. John Leonard Stroehlein was the owner of the house during those years. Notice the two little children peering out of the second-story window. This picture was taken before Mr. Oglebay made his additions. The mansion was added to the National Register of Historic Places in 1979. Compare the porch and windows with the next photograph.

MANSION, NOW, C. 1950. The Mansion Museum today is just as busy as it has ever been, with daily tours through the beautiful period rooms, which educate visitors about different times in the history of Wheeling. The wallpaper in the dining room was made by Zuber Company in France. The pattern is called "El Dorado." The chandelier was made in Wheeling by Hobbs, Brockunier, and Company in the 1870s. This colorful room played host to many of Wheeling's social elite. In 1972, the Mansion Museum became the first museum in West Virginia to be accredited by the American Association of Museums.

FESTIVAL OF LIGHTS, THEN. In 1985, Oglebay Park began the Festival of Lights Celebration, which covered 125 acres along a three-mile drive. The Wheeling Park Commission's creative director, Robert J. Otten, and world-renowned landscape lighting expert Dick Bosch were the designers of the original show. Mr. Otten designed the first five displays in 1985 and went on to create 42 additional attractions in Oglebay Park. Oglebay Park has received permission from the Charles M. Schulz Creative Associates to design light displays using some of the popular Peanuts characters.

FESTIVAL OF LIGHTS, NOW. The Oglebay Festival of Lights/City of Lights Celebration has grown by leaps and bounds over the years and is now considered to be the largest holiday lighting attraction in the United States. The festival now covers more than 300 acres over a six-mile drive. The festival has earned a permanent spot on the American Bus Association's Top International Events. Some of the more popular displays are the Teddy Bear Cartwheels, the Snowflake Tunnel, the Twelve Days of Christmas, and Skiing under the Polyhedron Star.

PARK TRANSPORTATION, THEN. Earl Oglebay is seen here inspecting his Waddington Farm, *c.* 1910. He was definitely a hands-on owner, who conducted daily inspections of his gardens and fields. Look closely at the thin wheel on this vehicle.

PARK TRANSPORTATION, NOW. The Oglebay shuttle carries visitors throughout the park in air-conditioned comfort. The sugar maple trees in the background are particularly beautiful in the autumn.

RIDING, THEN. This 1930s postcard states that this woman is a member of the Saddle Club. The idea for the Oglebay Riding Academy came in 1929 when an English coachman started the Saddle Club with only a few experienced equestrians and 10 horses. The Junior Saddle Club was organized in 1949 and came under the supervision of the Oglebay riding master.

RIDING, NOW. This photograph shows Jeanette Gue, owner of the Black Diamond Stables, riding Heidi in front of the old horse barn. There are currently nine horses in the stable. The complex contains an indoor arena, an outdoor arena, a warm-up ring, three pastures, two miles of trails, a back barn, a main stable, and a turn-out area. The stables still offer riding lessons and trail rides to the public. A ride on the trail takes approximately 50 minutes.

CABIN, THEN. The original cabins were built by skilled workers with the help of the CCC. The CCC workers received $21 a month plus room and board. The 75 CCC workers were under the care of Homer Fish, superintendent of Oglebay Park. He deserves a lot of credit for synchronizing the many workers with the myriad of tasks that needed to be accomplished.

COTTAGE, NOW. This is a photograph of the executive retreat, Waddington House. This modern complex was constructed in 1974 by Earl Oglebay's grandson, Courtney Burton Jr., for his family's personal use and has been renovated to include five bedrooms and dining facilities for 12 people. The Waddington House is one of 49 cottages scattered throughout Oglebay Park.

WILSON HALL, THEN. This was the first restaurant at Oglebay Park. It was originally a dairy farm. Wilson Hall also served as a meeting site for many local social groups. Wilson Hall burned to the ground in 1945.

HESS SHELTER, NOW. The Hess Children's Shelter was constructed on the site of the old Wilson Hall. It includes this large group shelter and the Wagon Shed. The students in the photograph are playing Frisbee football.

QUADRANGLE, THEN. The horse stables were built in 1905. These Hackney horses were the pride of Earl Oglebay.

CARRIAGE HOUSE GLASS, NOW. The Oglebay Institute Carriage House Glass Museum displays over 3,000 examples of glass made in Wheeling from 1829 to 1939. The top floor features glass products from West Virginia companies. It also contains the famous Sweeney Punch Bowl, which is the largest piece of cut lead glass ever made. Jim Helms and Bob Allen give demonstrations of glass blowing in the basement.

PALM ROOM, THEN, c. 1910. This view of an Oglebay gardener and the lush Palm Room shows how interested Earl Oglebay was in collecting and experimenting with exotic plants.

PALM ROOM, NOW. Nicholas and Grant Parshall enjoyed some exuberant flag waving in the Palm Room on April 8, 2005. These twins were visiting their grandmother, Thyra Parshall, who is the current president of the Wheeling Civic Garden Center executive board of directors. The twins' father, Staff Sgt. Steve Parshall, is currently fighting insurgents in Fallujah, Iraq.

FISHING, NOW. From left to right, Rudy Agras, Mike Carney, and Greg Carney are delighting in their first catch at Schenk Lake. They are the third generation to fish at this spot. These boys would agree with the *Cleveland Press* when it called Oglebay Park "a great place."